Contents

Some words are shown in bold, **like this**. You can find out what they mean by looking in the glossary.

What is citizenship?

Citizenship is about being a member of a group such as a family, a school, or a country. A citizen has **rights** and **responsibilities**. Having rights means there are certain ways that other people should treat you.

There are some things you can only do together as a group.

Exploring Citizenship

Good Relationships

Vic Parker

Raintree
SCHOOLS LIBRARY SERVICE

www.raintreepublishers.co.uk
Visit our website to find out more information about Raintree books.

To order:
☎ Phone 0845 6044371
🖷 Fax +44 (0) 1865 312263
🖳 Email myorders@raintreepublishers.co.uk

Customers from outside the UK please telephone +44 1865 312262

Raintree is an imprint of Capstone Global Library Limited, a company incorporated in England and Wales having its registered office at 7 Pilgrim Street, London, EC4V 6LB - Registered company number: 6695582

Text © Capstone Global Library Limited 2010
First published in hardback in 2010
Paperback edition first published in 2011

Edited by Charlotte Guillain and Catherine Veitch
Designed by Ryan Frieson and Betsy Wernert
Picture research by Elizabeth Alexander and Rebecca Sodergren
Production by Duncan Gilbert
Originated by Heinemann Library
Printed in China by South China Printing Company Ltd

ISBN 978 0 431 02536 0 (hardback)
14 13 12 11 10
10 9 8 7 6 5 4 3 2 1

ISBN 978 1 406 24720 6 (paperback)
15 14 13 12 11
10 9 8 7 6 5 4 3 2

British Library Cataloguing in Publication Data
Parker, Victoria
Good relationships. – (Exploring citizenship)

A full catalogue record for this book is available from the British Library.

Acknowledgements
We would like to thank the following for permission to reproduce photographs: Alamy **pp. 16** (© Jupiterimages/Bananastock), **26** (© Chris Rout); Corbis **pp. 7** (© Liba Taylor), **8** (© Hill Street Studios), **12** (© Heide Benser/zefa), **14** (© LWA-Dann Tardif/zefa), **17** (© Randy faris), **20** (© Image 100), **23** (© Jim Craigmyle), **24** (© Image Source), **29** (© Tom Stewart); Getty Images **pp. 6** (Eric Larrayadieu/Stone), **15** (Anthony Marsland/Riser), **18** (Victoria Blackie/Photographer's Choice), **22** (Stephen Simpson/Taxi); PA Photos **pp. 5** (Steve Parsons/PA Archive), **21** (Claire Deprez/REPORTER); Photolibrary **pp. 9** (Polka Dot Images/IT Stock), **10** (Odilon Dimier/Zen Shui), **11** (Tim Pannell/Flirt Collection), **27** (Radius Images); Shutterstock **pp. 4** (© Morgan Lane Photography), **19** (© Galina Barskaya).

Cover photograph of children laughing reproduced with permission of Corbis (© Kevin Dodge).

We would like to thank Yael Biederman for her help in the preparation of this book.

Every effort has been made to contact copyright holders of material reproduced in this book. Any omissions will be rectified in subsequent printings if notice is given to the publishers.

All the Internet addresses (URLs) given in this book were valid at the time of going to press. However, due to the dynamic nature of the Internet, some addresses may have changed, or sites may have changed or ceased to exist since publication. While the author and publisher regret any inconvenience this may cause readers, no responsibility for any such changes can be accepted by either the author or the publisher.

Having responsibilities means you should act or behave in a certain way. The way you behave affects other people. At home and in school you have rights and responsibilities.

You can be responsible for other people's safety.

What are relationships?

Every day, you meet lots of people, such as your family, friends, and neighbours. You spend time with your teacher and other adults at school. There are other people who help you in places such as at a doctor's surgery or in shops.

When you go shopping, there are people who help you. It is important to help them, too.

Your closest relationships might be with your family or with friends.

A relationship is how you get on with people around you and how they get on with you. If you have a bad relationship with someone, it can make you feel worried and upset. However, if you have a good relationship with someone, you will both feel happier.

Good family relationships

You and your family will celebrate many special occasions together.

Your family is the people you live with. All families are different. Families can include a mother, a father, a stepmother or stepfather, brothers and sisters, a grandmother or grandfather, an aunt or uncle, foster parents, or the other adults and children.

The people in a family may spend a lot of time together. For everyone to get on well, family members should treat each other with **respect**. If an adult in your family asks you to do something, it is usually for a good reason.

The adults in your family want you to be safe and happy.

Living together

The members of a family have to share living space and things. Nobody likes to have their toys or clothes used by other people without them asking first. In order to have good family relationships, everyone must **respect** other people's things.

If you treat other people's things with respect, they are more likely to let you borrow them.

In a family's home, there are always lots of jobs to be done, such as washing up, cleaning, and tidying up. If everyone takes **responsibility** for helping, these jobs will get done more quickly and easily. What other jobs could you help with around your home?

Helping at home can make you feel good.

Time together, time alone

Everybody in a family likes doing different things, such as reading, playing games, or watching television. While it is fun to do things alone, it can sometimes be more fun to find something that everyone in the family can do together.

A picnic can be enjoyable for everyone.

We all like to spend quiet time on our own sometimes, too. It is an important way to think and relax. Try not to disturb anyone who wants to be alone for a while. What do you like doing best by yourself?

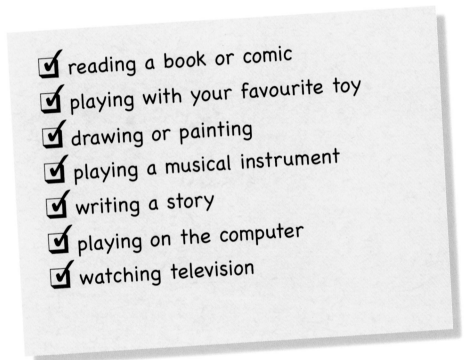

☑ reading a book or comic
☑ playing with your favourite toy
☑ drawing or painting
☑ playing a musical instrument
☑ writing a story
☑ playing on the computer
☑ watching television

Think about it

How do you feel when you want to be alone and people disturb you?

Good relationships at school

All the adults at school want to help you to do your best.

At school, your teacher helps you all day. There are other adults who help you at school, such as classroom and playground assistants. You can help them in turn by listening carefully, being polite, and always trying to do your best.

You can often help out in the classroom.

The adults at school might sometimes need help, too. When you offer to help them, you are showing them **respect**. Also, if you offer to do a job at school, it shows that you are caring and **responsible**.

What is friendship?

Friendship is a relationship with someone you care about a lot and enjoy being with, and they feel the same way about you. Some people have lots of friends while other people have just one or two special friends.

Friends like spending time together.

Good friends like to share things.

Good friends think about each other and care about each other. Here are some ways to be an excellent friend. Can you think of more?

Good friends:

☑ listen to their friends' thoughts and ideas

☑ take turns

☑ ask how their friends feel

☑ cheer up their friends if they are having a bad time

☑ **praise** their friends when they do something well.

17

Staying friends

To have a good relationship with a friend, you should treat them as you would like them to treat you. This means that sometimes you should put them first. For example, sometimes you could offer to play your friend's favourite game. It is fine for friends to have different **opinions**, but it is important to try not to argue.

Friends can feel differently about things sometimes.

All people sometimes do things that upset others. You may sometimes say something nasty to your friends or be mean to them. It is important to think about what you have done and why it is wrong. If you say sorry, and try really hard not to do the same thing again, it can make everyone feel better.

Friends say sorry and forgive each other.

Being a friendly person

You have to work together with different people in many different places.

It is a good idea to be friendly to everyone, not just the people you like the most. This is because there are times when people all need to work together as a team to do a good job. This is called **cooperation**.

If you leave someone out of a game or in the classroom, they might feel sad or angry. You can make friends by asking to help them, or offering to share something.

How do you feel if other people are not friendly to you?

Good relationships out and about

When you are out and about, you can look for ways to help the people you are with. For example, you could offer to carry a bag for a parent. Or you could bend down and pick up something that has been dropped.

When you wait your turn, you are helping other people.

Help your doctor by listening hard and speaking clearly.

Whenever you go to places where you meet new people, you should try to be polite and helpful. This way, everyone should be polite and helpful to you, too.

Talking and listening

People who care about you will often ask you to tell them about your ideas and the things you like and do not like. Do not forget to ask questions about them, too. Taking turns to talk is what makes a good relationship.

Listening is as important as talking.

It is great to talk, but it is also good to listen to what others say. People often have great ideas that you will miss if you do not listen to them. Here are a few things that make someone a good listener. Can you think of more?

A good listener:

- ☑ looks at the person speaking
- ☑ does not rush the person speaking
- ☑ does not interrupt
- ☑ does not do something else at the same time as listening
- ☑ does not fidget.

Think about it

How do you feel when you are telling a friend something important and they do not listen to you?

Good relationships in bad times

Sometimes if we feel worried or upset about something, we might get grumpy with other people and may not feel like talking to them. This can make them feel upset, too. Instead, try to share your problems with the people who care about you. They might know how to make you feel better, and it could also make them feel happy to help you.

A hug can often make you feel much better.

If someone feels poorly, you can cheer them up.

See if you can spot the next time someone else feels sad. How could what you do and say make them feel? What can you do to help them to feel better?

Good relationships and happiness

It is important to have good relationships so that you and others are happy together. Others will help and be kind to you if you are kind to them.

To have a good relationship, you should:

- ☑ help people and let them help you
- ☑ be **honest**
- ☑ listen to other people's **opinions**
- ☑ think about another person's point of view
- ☑ **respect** other people's **property**
- ☑ put other people first sometimes
- ☑ be willing to learn from others.

Having good relationships will make your life more interesting and more fun. You will be happier and so will other people.

Playing games is a great way to build good relationships.

Glossary

cooperation working together

honest truthful, able to be trusted

opinion point of view, thoughts about something or someone

praise say to someone how well they have done

property something that belongs to someone

respect way of treating someone or something with kindness, politeness, and care

responsibility something that it is your job to do as a good and helpful member of a group

right how you should be treated by others, in a way that is thought to be good or fair by most people

Find out more

Books

Citizenship: Being Fair, Cassie Mayer (Heinemann Library, 2007)

Citizenship: Being Helpful, Cassie Mayer (Heinemann Library, 2007)

Citizenship: Making Friends, Cassie Mayer (Heinemann Library, 2007)

Start-Up Citizenship: A Diverse World, Louise and Richard Spilsbury (Evans Brothers, 2007)

Start-Up Citizenship: Taking Part, Louise and Richard Spilsbury (Evans Brothers, 2007)

Website

www.gogivers.org
This animated site shows children what it means to be part of a caring society.

Index